W9-CRU-961

The Gospel Priesthood

Publisher's Note

Born in the year 1905 in the land of Egypt – "the land which for a time sheltered Abraham, Joseph, Moses and Jeremias," Hubert van Zeller was particularly interested in Sacred Scripture and desired to get Catholics to read the Bible. This he would do starting in 1935 with a series of full-length biographies on Biblical figures.

After becoming a Benedictine monk in 1924 and being ordained a priest in 1930, Father van Zeller began his prodigious literary writings in earnest. His first book was on the twelve minor prophets and was followed by *Sackcloth and Ashes* in 1937. Then from his sick bed he wrote *Isaias: Man of Ideas* (1938). Good reviews encouraged him to follow this up in 1942 with *Daniel: Man of Desires*, *Jeremias: Man of Tears,* which was chosen the book of the month by the Catholic Book Club. Next came *Ezechiel: Man of Signs* (1944) and two prayer books, *Lord God* for boys and *Come Lord* for girls.

In addition to his many Scriptural works, Father van Zeller wrote *Liturgical Asides* (1939) and several novels and plays under the pseudonym Hugh Venning.

The Gospel Priesthood

Exhortations on the pastoral vocation

Dom Hubert van Zeller

Roman Catholic Books

Post Office Box 2286, Fort Collins, CO 80522
booksforcatholics.com

Nihil obstat: D. Ricardvs Davey
Censor Depvtatvs Cong. Anglo-Ben.
Imprimatvr: H.K. Byrne
AB. Praes. Cong. Anglo-Ben.
Die XXV Martii MCMLV

———————————

Nihil obstat: Joannes M.T. Barton, S.T.D., L.S.S.
Censor Depvtatvs
Imprimatvr: E. Morrogh Bernard
Vicarivs Generalis
Westmonasterii: Die V Jvlii MCMLV

ISBN 1-929291-33-7

DEDICATED TO

FATHER MICHAEL DRISCOLL

CONTENTS

PREFACE

THIS book represents a series of articles which appeared in *Emmanuel* throughout the year 1954, and it is by the generous permission of Father Raymond Tartre, the Editor, that they are reproduced here. In writing them it was the purpose to cover the liturgical year, taking the dominant idea of the month or season, and applying some of the liturgy's more practical principles to one or other aspect of the priestly vocation. It might be felt that though this may work well enough when the articles are read at monthly intervals, it must make for confusion when the mysteries of the year are taken in one piece. It would—if the programme were strictly followed. Thus it has here to be admitted that the frame set by the Ordo and the Missal has been made deliberately flexible: thoughts besides those suggested by the appropriate season or feast have been developed. The priest-reader who is envisaged is not the harassed preacher who finds himself hunting at the last moment for something which will do for a sermon;

it is the humble soul who is looking for something which will stir a desire for prayer. The reflections contained in the pages which follow are designed to awaken dormant or deluded consciences. That is why they are written in the form of thrusts, of jabs from the short sword. That is why the book is a slim one. That is why a day of recollection, rather than a full-length retreat, is probably the more suitable occasion for its use.

Finally it is to be hoped that the presumption of a religious who dares to write for the enlightenment of diocesan clergy may be forgiven: the undertaking would never have been begun had not the invitation from without been as pressing as it was.

1

THE ESSENTIAL PRIESTHOOD

IN most countries the cry is raised about the shortage of vocations to the priesthood. The first need, however, is not for more priests but for holier priests. A lowering in the level of sanctity is obviously a greater menace to the Church than a reduction of numbers. One reason for this is that whereas recruitment depends entirely upon the Holy Spirit—and we can always count upon the Holy Spirit to safeguard the necessary work of the Church by calling enough men into the ministry to do it—the standard of fidelity to the vocation, on the other hand, is to a large extent a matter of personal determination. The priest, under the operation of grace but with his own very individual responsibility, fashions the shape of his priestly sanctity. It is the nature of this sanctity, and the obligation relating to it, that will form the material of this series of considerations.

The priestly vocation is, in essence, twofold:

its end is personal sanctification and the salvation of souls. The priesthood, though complete in itself, does not exist for its own sake but for the redemp' tion of mankind. It exactly follows the pattern of the priesthood of Christ: worship through union with the Father's will, redemption through sacri' fice. To say this is not to say anything original— it is probably the answer which every priest would give to the question 'what are priests really for?'— but because so much connected with the ministry inclines us to forget it, it is a truth which we priests have need to remember. 'The first function of the priest has for its object the *corpus Christi verum*,' says St. Thomas, 'the second the *corpus Christi mysticum*.'[1] Men are ordained not to make good use of their abilities, not to maintain them' selves in a congenial way of life, not to be builders or writers or preachers or theologians, but to be men who will lay down leisure and life in reclaim' ing, with Christ, the world from sin. The vocation, to see it in a slightly different light, is not only to say Mass, to be faithful in the practice of mental prayer and the recitation of the Divine Office— vital as it is that these things be given primacy of

[1]*Sum. Theol.*, Suppl. Q. xxxvi, art. ii, ad 1.

place—but to give the Christ-life to souls. 'For them do I sanctify myself': the Christ-life lived, the Christ-life spread—and in that order.

Is this to pitch the ideal too high? Read the prayers in the ritual for the ordination of priests. Read the First Epistle to Timothy, chapter four. Take the words 'apostle,' 'minister,' 'pastor,' and get down to what they really mean. Leave aside for a moment the more comfortable associations which have gathered round the idea of the priest-hood; forget the allowances which are made by the charitable laity; dismiss the kind of excuse which we priests make for ourselves when we compare our own way of life with that either of worldlings or of other priests in other countries or other periods of history. Yes, yes, we may be living in exceptional times, we may have to find a new technique, we may be saints without knowing it, but what, to get down to it, is the idea in every-body's mind at the mention of *priest*? The Buddhist conception would be not much different. The man of prayer, the man who spends himself for the love of God. To the heathen and the

heretic, the idea is the same. Whatever the doctrine, whatever the discipline, the essence of the
thing is perfectly clear. All that we Catholic
priests have to ask ourselves is 'how do I fit into
that?' If I have any other idea of it I have got the
priesthood wrong, and must think again. I must
re-cast myself, my ordained self, anew. The
Catholic priest, like the Catholic Church, must be
holy and apostolic—in that order. It is not enough
that he receives his orders, in lineal descent, from
the authority of the Apostles: he must *be* an
apostle. It is not enough that he be one with his
fellow Catholics by virtue of allegiance, sacra-
ments, and belief: he must be one with the tradition of the Church's holiness. Indeed it is difficult
to see how a priest can come anywhere near to the
fulfilment of his vocation unless the marks of the
Church are at the same time the target of his own
endeavour.

IF our vocation is to be viewed in the light of what
has just been said, we might choose as a suitable
background for the investigation of its responsibilities the liturgical cycle of feasts and seasons. Such

an approach should, properly, start with a review of the priesthood in relation to Advent; since, however, it is probably more convenient to follow the ordinary rather than the liturgical calendar—the *Ordo Divini Officii* is, after all, issued at the end of December and not, as would be more liturgically fitting, at the end of November—we open with the Epiphany and January.

Epiphania: manifestation. Three distinct 'manifestations': *Trium miraculis ornatum diem sanctum colimus: hodie stella Magos duxit ad praesepium; hodie vinum ex aqua factum est ad nuptias; hodie in Jordane a Joanne Christus baptizari voluit.* There is enough in each aspect of this threefold feast to provide us with material for an entire retreat.

For the feast and its octave we have a glittering array of Fathers to act as commentators. It is unfortunate that to many priests the nocturn lessons in the breviary are so many cross-bars in a hurdle race. In the effort to reach the finish, or even in the effort to reach the next group of psalms where we feel we are on the flat again, we skim lightly over the particular Doctor of the moment. Sometimes, particularly if he is one of the Greek Fathers rendered precisely into Latin, we do not even pay him the compliment of studying him as a hurdle: we use our professional licence, and run through. The Fathers chosen by the Church to proclaim the mysteries of the Epiphany are Saints Leo, Gregory, Augustine, Jerome and Ambrose. But if the nocturn lessons are felt to be either too formid-able or too familiar, we have modern writers who can provide us with material not only for prayer (which is the main thing) but also for the particular kind of inquiry and speculation which it was the function of the ancients to pro-mote. Read for example what Bishop Sheen has to say about the Epiphany in the opening chapters of his *Eternal Galilean*.

'For the priest and religious there is no middle course. It is either perfection—at least desired and pursued, if not actually acquired—or progressive decline.' And this from Cardinal Lavigerie: 'If the search for perfection is fundamental to the priest's vocation, the offering of self is its primary expres-sion.' Gold, frankincense, myrrh. The formula of self-oblation springs readily enough to the lips, but, having made the grand gesture of handing our-selves over to God, are we quite so ready to let

Him have the freedom of the things that we possess? Do we give tithes to God, but rather larger tithes to comfort, entertainment, private interest? Leaving the other two aspects of the Epiphany Feast to be considered on an ensuing page, we have here the searching business of our expenditures to review. 'But,' it will be objected, 'you are meant to be telling me how to be a good priest . . . and you talk about accounts.' Father, be honest. Can you sincerely claim to be building the house of the spirit—while the temporal house doesn't bear looking into? *Hostiam puram, hostiam sanctam, hostiam immaculatam*: here is your cue to what you became on your ordination day . . . and to what you are called to renew when you kneel in spirit with the wise men at the yearly repetition of the Epiphany.

2

THE IDENTIFIED PRIESTHOOD

THE thought of Christ present in the poor is familiar enough. That He is more particularly present in the priest is often overlooked. The imprisoned, the hungry, the sick : 'as long as you did it to one of these My least brethren you did it to Me.' Nothing could be more clear. If the presence of Christ in His priests is less clear, may it not be that this particular kind of identification has never been fully learned? We know the texts : 'he that heareth you heareth Me . . . whose sins you shall forgive they are forgiven . . . do this in commemoration of Me . . . feed My sheep . . . as My Father hath sent Me so I also send you . . . go ye and teach all nations . . .' But perhaps we feel that possessing Him so, we are getting Him less immediately than if we were sick or imprisoned or without shelter. Perhaps in the back of our minds lurks the thought that the words of our

Lord just quoted were addressed to 'the Church,' to 'the bishops,' and that we are getting the benefit of them at one or two removes. We have inherited, yes, the grace of Christ's priestly presence, but more (we feel) by delegation than by our Lord's individual act of identification. To see it thus is to see it incompletely.

'In virtue of the priesthood of Christ,' writes Père Bourgoing, the Oratorian who edited the works of Cardinal Bérulle, 'we priests are clothed with the very Person of Christ: we speak, we act, we con´ secrate as though we were His very self.' Thus if the needy are extensions of Christ in need, the clergy are extensions of Christ ministering to those in need. It is not even as if Christ, the first priest of the New Law, projected Himself into the labours of priests who were to come after Him, sanctifying, for example, our own ministry from the distance of nearly two thousand years. He does much more than this. He shares His priesthood with us *now*. It is all in the present tense. He is identified with the priesthood which operates through me. 'Priests are the express form and

B

figure of Christ,' writes M. Olier in his *Traités des Saintes Ordres,* 'and so should reveal the form of Christ in themselves.' And again, 'the priest is in the Church like a living Jesus Christ; and a Jesus Christ as Head of His Church.'

THE doctrine of the Indwelling, applying to all baptized souls who are in a state of grace, finds an altogether fuller interpretation in the case of the priest. The man who can say every morning 'this is My Body . . . this is My Blood' is personified in Christ: he is saying more than his own human individuality would entitle him to say. In a very real way the priest should be able to claim with St. Paul, 'I live now not I but Christ lives in me.' And if this be so he can go on to proclaim that 'I work now not I but Christ works in me; I pray now not I but Christ prays in me; I love, suffer, make decisions and take responsibilities, now not I but Christ who develops His life within me. He does all these things through the me-that-was, and that is now trying more and more to recast himself in the image and likeness of his Model.'

Thus it is not only when the priest is at the altar

or in the confessional that the Person of Christ catches him up into Himself. The process is continual. It is intensified according to the soul's union with God in prayer; it is interrupted by sin. If the priest makes himself worthy of the relationship, he ends up a saint; if he neglects its implications, he endangers his salvation. Like perfection itself, it invites a never ceasing surrender to grace, a progressive readiness to meet the unfolding of the will of God.

SINCE the identification of Christ with the priestly character is a relationship and not just a trick of the intellect—since it is a habit of soul and a positive fact—it does not depend upon whether the priest happens to be thinking of it at the time. The priest may forget about it while he is performing his duties as a priest. The relationship goes on, giving direction to his act. In the case of the saints the relationship is dominant the whole time: the saints may be said to live more or less in the awareness of it. To them it finds its fulfilment in perfect love, and 'to them that love God all things work together for good.' For them there is the spiral ascent whereby inward love prompts acts of outward charity, which, in their turn, bring fuel for further fires of inward love. So much for the saint. What of the would-be saint, the man who is not so sure about this spiral ascent? What of the average priest (if there be such a person) like you and me? The process may be less easy to trace, but the principle is the same. To them that love God less, but love Him nevertheless and are faith-ful to their state in life, all things work together for good—but less effectively. Every work which is done in virtue of his priesthood is, whether the priest happens to be conscious of it or not, made holy. A good act performed by a priest is, by reason of his share in the priesthood of Christ, more sanctifying than the same act performed by a layman. An evil act all the more condemning. With a deepening of the spiritual life engendered by the grace of ordination, the soul of the priest comes gradually to produce all his operations after the model and under the impulse of Christ. At the same time it must be remembered that spirals can work downwards as well as upwards.

THE mysteries of the Epiphany which still remain to be considered may be found to take on new significance when examined in the light of the above.

First, then, Christ at the marriage feast in Cana. Here we have a gathering which was part religious and part social. Commentators tell us that there were several reasons why our Lord worked this particular miracle at this particular time. He was bearing Divine witness to the sanctity of marriage; He was sparing the purely natural shame of His host, and so providing us with an example of thoughtfulness and charity; He was preparing Galilee for the campaign of teaching which He was about to launch, and, with a wider public in view, providing precedent for the changing of one sub-stance into another. If water into wine, why not wine into His own precious blood? Thus far the commentators. But an application which we priests might do well to dwell upon is this: Christ's attendance at semi-religious and semi-social occa-sions as reflected in our own duties of the same kind. Do our so-called priestly engagements relate sufficiently to the priesthood? Is our manner, while we are engaged in these affairs, of Christ or of the world? Leaving the question of recreation proper to be dealt with on a later page, we are here considering those secular contacts to which our ministry directly renders us liable. They either bring us nearer to God or draw us further away. Designed for our advancement and for the advancement of others, these opportunities can never be entirely neutral in effect.

In his novel *The Woman who was Poor* Léon Bloy makes one of the characters tell a story about the Cana wedding. A guest, a merchant of the tribe of Issachar, sensing the possibility of hidden powers in the wine that had been water, and noting that more was provided than was necessary for the feast, made an offer to the host and bought up the remainder. At intervals during the next three years this wine was sipped, rousing each time the mood of rebellion. It was this same wine which, on the night of Maundy Thursday, inflamed the minds of those who mingled with the crowds later on and shouted 'Crucify Him.' There is much about our priesthood which is like the wine in Bloy's legend. And this is only what you would expect when Christ Himself 'is set for the fall and resurrection of many in Israel.'

Then there is the third of the Epiphany mysteries : Jesus is baptized by John in the Jordan. In the anointing of the priest the Fathers see another and a mystical baptism. As Christ rose from the Jordan to begin His ministry so the priest re-dedicates himself to his baptism's promise. The dedication is sealed, consecrated, ratified by the Father and Holy Spirit. From now on we are other Christs. 'This is My beloved Son.'

3

THE MORTIFIED PRIESTHOOD

WITH Lent comes the need to review the priest's attitude towards the whole range of self-denial: its necessity, its purity of intention, its practical expression. There is nothing related to the priestly life—not even prayer—which is so easily explained away as the duty of doing penance. Yet there can hardly be anything more obvious than the association in the mind between Head and members of the mystical body: 'If the Head be crowned with thorns,' says St. Augustine, 'the body must suffer correspondingly.' The priesthood, if it be Christ's, is the priesthood of self-sacrifice. 'Your Lord is pierced with nails,' says St. John Chrysostom, 'and do you live in luxury? Is this the act of the generous fighter?' It is the glory of the Christian priesthood that this specific quality of sharing in the sacrifice by co-oblation is something proper to ourselves, something left undeveloped in earlier cults. In the ancient religions, even in the Old Law itself, the priest is seen as one who stands at the altar: he offers, he prays, he slays: he is not thought of as part of the sacrifice itself. In the Christian priesthood there is not this division.

THE man who celebrates Mass is, mystically and figuratively but nevertheless significantly, on the paten at the *Suscipe* and in the chalice at the *Offerimus*. When the words of consecration are pronounced it is the priest's as well as Christ's body that is being re-dedicated to the praise of the Father. And at that level the priest is invited to live his life. It would be a mistake to think of our Mass and our position in it as separated into parts: I, the man, as the subject; the sacred species, the material element, as the object; God, Father and Son and Holy Ghost, as the end. But because Christ is at once priest, victim, and end of His own sacrifice, so we can think of ourselves, made one with Christ in His sacrificial act, as reflecting in our bodies and souls and outward lives the same continued immolation directed to-wards the same Father in the same redemptive act.

It follows from all this that penance of some sort, down-to-earth mortification, must find its essential place in our scheme for God's service. 'The sacrifice of Christ is not offered with the sanctity belonging to it,' says St. Cyprian, 'if our oblation does not correspond to His Passion.' The Fathers all say the same thing . . . and we, who are supposed not only to be their followers but who are supposed also—even to the extent of being called by the same name 'father'—to reflect their paternity towards souls, tone down their doctrine about voluntary asceticism until there is practically nothing left of it.

BUT even if Christ were never to demand the co-operation of His priests in the self-surrender of the Mass, it would still be the function of the priest to do penance for himself and for mankind. '*Parce, Domine, parce populo tuo*' cry the priests, as we are reminded on Ash Wednesday from the prophet Joel, '*immutemur habitu in cinere et cilicio: jejune-mus et ploremus ante Dominum quia multum misericors est dimittere peccata nostra.*' It is for the priest to be the go-between, the mediator. Who can look Joel's exhortations in the face? How many of us dare study the *whole* liturgy of Ash Wednesday and Good Friday? To remind our flocks that they are dust and into dust they shall return calls for no great effort on our part; to kneel three times while creeping to the Cross on the annual celebration of Christ's death calls for no great effort on our part; but it does rather go against our comfort-loving selves to say *and mean* 'let us amend for the better . . . let us fast and lament.' At least during the weeks of Lent there should be a serious response to this challenge, a practical realization of the more salty element of our vocation as being the most appropriate reflection of His own essential manifestation to the world.

If, then, penance is an integral part of the vocation, the next question is how is it to be done? 'We are called by God to labour at a masterpiece; the training of a good priest is a master work—so difficult and lofty that only God Himself can carry it to effect.' This is from St. Vincent de Paul, and it shows us the source of our penitential impulse. The first condition of true penance is dependence upon grace. Christian mortification is supernatural and positive or it is nothing. Natural asceticism, physical toughness, might of itself be more of an obstacle than a help : it could well lead to ruthlessness, pride, hardness. Those penitential practices which do not bind the soul closer to Christ's Passion are not of the least use either to the soul or to God. If the act of penance is not at the same time a virtual act of prayer—that is to say a work directed in the will towards God's glory—it is much better left alone. (This is not to claim that throughout the renunciation, any more than throughout the set exercise of prayer, the mind must be fixed upon God. The word 'virtual,' included above, must be considered.) Renuncia-tions undertaken for motives other than the love of God are spiritually so much dead wood. 'When you fast, be not as the hypocrites . . . when you give alms, let not your left hand know what the right hand does . . . lay not up to yourselves treasures on earth.' This is told us on the first day of Lent; there is no excuse for getting our motives and direction wrong.

TURNING now to the third problem—the practical one of what penances to adopt—we have to allow that not all priests have the health for the complete Lenten fast as it appears in the books. Reluctantly the allowance is made, because again and again it is found that a generous attempt to keep the Church's traditional Lenten observance is aided in a quite remarkable way by grace, and that men of frail constitution but determined purpose can do violence to themselves during Lent without any of the harmful results which might be expected to follow at other times of the year. Two or three days in each week would hardly tax the body: it is the idea of the fast, not the actual observance, which is the main difficulty. And if prayer can strengthen the body it can also strengthen the mind: we ought to be able to get over obstacles which are ideas only.

A GENERATION of lay people is growing up which scarcely knows what the Church requires at this season of Lent: it should be for the clergy not merely to tell the people but to show the people. An immortified clergy, however skilled in theology and pulpit oratory, can never truly shepherd the flock, can never really drive home the lessons of the Gospel. For the layman to notice that the whole year through, even during Lent, his priest smokes, eats, drinks, spends money on sport and entertainment as lavishly as he himself does cannot but be disedifying. When the standard of living is noticeably higher in the presbytery than in the rest of the parish the disedification can amount to scandal. The priest is meant to rise above luxury, must train himself to be indifferent to (even a little scornful of) personal comfort, should give a lead in the procession towards Calvary. A priest is, after all, a leader. Not for him to sit behind closed shutters and control by telephone. 'And no man should dare to become a leader of others,' says Dionysius the Areopagite, 'unless in all his habits he be deiform and godlike.' Denis may be thought to set too high a standard, but even St. Thomas, who is certainly more down to earth than Dionysius, says that priests 'must shine before men by their goodness.' Sad indeed if all that the flock sees of its shepherd is his mastery of worldly affairs and his assurance in worldly society.

To conclude. The priest may not be departmental in his relationship to Christ and Christ's members. He cannot choose to follow Christ in His preaching but not in His suffering, to worship His Incarnation but neglect His act of Redemption, to preach His Transfiguration and not to practise His doctrine of the Cross, to follow Him in His charity but not in His Gethsemani. The disciple must be as His master, the servant as His lord. If Christ is the Divine Mediator, the priest is the divinely appointed human mediator. 'The function of a priest is to be a mediator . . . that ministry is spiritual to which priests are vowed, and by which they are constituted mediators between God and the world.' Where there is no penance there can be no true mediation.

4

THE RISEN PRIESTHOOD

THE life of the priest, indeed the life of every
Christian but more especially the life of the
priest, should be based upon the Holy Week
sequence of Good Friday, Holy Saturday, Easter
Sunday. With Christ the priest accepts suffering,
dies to sin, rises above the world in the new life of
grace. Each stage, each movement towards the ulti-
mate triumph, is necessary : without the endurance
and the death, the drawn-out defeat cannot be
turned into the climax of victory. Mystically, the
priesthood must follow the life of Christ, the death
of Christ, the resurrection of Christ. The liturgy
which proclaims these mysteries is not a piece of
historical pageantry; it is doctrine, it is fact, it is
as peremptory a statement as a notice pinned on a
board. The cycle of feasts, and among them more
significantly those that move from Passion Sunday
to the Paschal season, are not the expression of a
literary fancy but are as practical as a bishop's

pastoral and as searching as an examination of conscience. They *are* an examination of conscience.

'You are dead and your life is hid with Christ in
God . . . with Christ I am nailed to the cross
. . . our former nature has been crucified with
Him . . . and if we have died with Christ, we
have faith to believe that we shall share His life
. . . we have been buried with Him, died with
Him, that so, just as Christ was raised from the
dead, we, too, might live and move in a new kind
of existence.' These scattered quotations from St.
Paul (Colossians, Galatians, Romans) combine to
stress the same staggering fact. The Epistle for the
Easter Midnight Mass states the Christian's duty
in two verses : 'If you be risen with Christ seek the
things that are above, where Christ is sitting at the
right hand of God : mind the things that are above,
not the things that are upon the earth.' We priests,
of all men, are made worthy to stand before
God without reproach. Christ has caught us up
to His side on the cross, has kept us close to His
lifeless body in the tomb, and now has given us, if
we accept the position in His terms, His own

c

mastery over the devil, the world, and the flesh.
For us there must be no room for evil, no com-
promise with the spirit of the world, none of those
tolerant little commonsense concessions to the con-
cupiscence of the body and the pride of life. Easter
Sunday restates the message of Jahveh to His
chosen followers: 'You shall be holy unto Me
because I the Lord am holy; and I have separated you from other people that you should be
mine.'

WE, like the sons of Levi and Aaron, are a race
apart, and only in the measure that we remain
apart, not trying to ape the ways of other tribes,
shall we be able either to bring souls to God or to
advance our own perfection. It is the standing
paradox of the apostolate that we help the world
most by being as little like it as possible. It is
equally the standing paradox of the spiritual life
that we help ourselves by denying ourselves. In the
last analysis the good that we do, both to others
and to our own souls, is measured by how closely
we conform to what we are meant to be in the
eyes of God. There is a pattern. We are men and

we are ordained: we have to be ourselves, as priests. This is how God sees us.

Our vocation then is in this sense twofold: we find our salvation at once by mixing with mankind and by being unworldly, by doing all in our power to draw mankind and by being ourselves with-drawn. Our problem, obviously, will be how to safeguard the side of our life which is reserved for God alone from a contamination which for most of us the circumstances of our ministry must in-evitably force upon us. How, without becoming a hermit, can I avoid becoming a worldling?

No priest could, left to himself, resolve without loss to one or other the apparently conflicting re-sponsibilities. But the whole point is that no priest *is* left to himself. Unless he dispenses with the extra dimension of grace, and unless he also rejects the helps which are essentially bound up with his state of life every priest is more than adequately equipped to meet precisely this twofold pull. It is in the terms of the contract. If the dual respon-sibility is the very stuff of his vocation, the grace to cope with it is equally so. 'The grace which is in him by the laying on of hands' can at any moment be stirred up.

Now this supernatural assistance need not be thought of as a *charisma*, an extraordinary power which comes to the priest who is faced with rival claims. It is not a tightrope-walker's gift, miraculously bestowed, enabling the priest to preserve his mental balance; it is the joint effect of ordination, confidence in God, and readiness to abide by the conditions of the life. It is not so much an act of faith which reconciles opposing loyalties as a habit of fidelity to grace which sees to it that neither loyalty goes unfulfilled. The soul who yields unconditionally to the mould of the priesthood has his approach indicated to him; his setting is fashioned for him as he goes along by the Providence of God.

In the development of God's plan through the Christian centuries the priesthood has acquired for itself a defensive armour against the assault of evil. Thus you have the recitation of the Divine Office, the submission to the bishop and the consequent dependence upon authority, the vow of chastity, the use of a distinctive dress, the various customs of the diocese relating to retreats and other occasions of association—all making up the protec' tive covering which shelters the essential vocation. Historically what has happened is that tradition has justified experiment, and authority has set its seal to tradition. Ecclesiastical discipline is a thing evolved. And evolved moreover not for the sake of discipline but for the sake of ecclesiastics. Evolved under God, and for the good of souls. Thus observ' ances which might look to be somewhat haphazard in the process of their formation are in fact seen to be, once they have taken authoritative shape, not natural contingencies at all but supernatural neces' sities. God has planned ecclesiastical discipline, just as He has planned the rules of religious orders, as providing the best setting for the risen Christian, for men who are to live above the world which it is their vocation to serve.

THERE may be nothing in the Scriptures about clergy retreats or wearing the clerical collar, but these things are to be taken seriously nevertheless. They, together with the other regulations, form part of the skin which is necessary to the growth of the fruit. For a fruitgrower to peel his oranges before removing them from the tree would be no less lunatic than for a priest to divest himself of the protective skin with which centuries of Christian practice have surrounded his priesthood. The fruit of a vocation is not meant to stand the strain of being peeled in mid-growth; it is entitled to its natural, and in this case its supernatural, safeguards. All the time the priest is growing in holiness, is developing in Christ, is putting on the new man. He dare not allow the common clay of his nature to be exposed.

When a priest, for example, assumes the disguise of a layman, he forfeits his right to a particular kind of spiritual protection. (I am not of course here considering the priest-worker movement, nor any other where the laying aside of clerical dress is sanctioned by episcopal authority.) Enjoying easier access to the hotel bar, mingling more unobtrusively in the country club, the priest in lay clothes has shed a skin which the soul may not be able to do without. The devil, noting that the defences are down, makes capital out of the transformation. The orange is hanging precariously . . . has already lost something of its freshness and its proper taste. 'Great spiritual wealth,' says St. Vincent de Paul, 'is only preserved with as much care as is devoted to great earthly possessions.' A priest will insure his car, take trouble to know all about his investments, make detailed provision for his vacation, and then go cheerfully risking his state of grace. This is the world all over. But the priest, like Christ Himself, is not of the world. Like Christ, the priest has triumphed over the world, and minds now the things that are above and not the things that are in the world.

5

THE COMPASSIONATE PRIESTHOOD

IT is the priest's job—since God, surveying His work, pronounced it good—to love as many of God's creatures as he can. With the eyes of faith he must look for what the poet or painter sees with the vision of his particular gift. And this is none too easy; it does not come to him naturally. But since it comes to him supernaturally, this new perspective should not be too difficult to cultivate. Once he has learned—and he can learn it only in the unremitting practice of prayer—to see God in creatures, he has found the answer to the main problem of his apostolate. Any man who loves all other men enough to treat them as God means them to be treated is in a fair way to becoming a saint. By the time he is a saint he sees creatures in God, which is something different again.

IF, then, the key to the priest's work for souls is seeing each individual as the reflection of Christ, the more he sees mankind—and particularly that

portion of it with which he has to deal—as indivi-
duals rather than as a crowd the better. God can
save mobs but we cannot. God can save mobs
because He does not have to look upon them as
mobs: He looks upon them as being a million
images of Himself. It is as an image of God that the
priest has to study and love every single soul who
comes his way. He will never serve his parish, or
his public, unless he serves the individual member
of it first. It is through the isolated soul—one
isolated soul after another—that we come to know
the race. We cannot love humanity as we are
meant to love it unless we love its single human
beings. If we think the individual is worthless it
means that we think the human race is worthless.
Mere quantity cannot give to man his importance
—either in the sight of God or in the sight of men.
If we want to serve humanity we must serve its
types. Not its sublimest types but its every-day
types. And we do not have to look far to find
them. Having found them, we see that they *are*
sublime.

In proportion as the world is viewed in God's perspective not only do souls appear in the likeness

of Christ but more and more does the soul viewing them take upon himself Christ's own attitude towards them. As Christ in the Garden of Geth' semani 'became sin' for man, so the priest in the development of his union with God by prayer and charity bears a share in Christ's vicarious guilt. The priest comes to know sin, not only as having himself sinned but, and far more comprehensively, as having 'put on Christ' who 'became sin' for man. The whole approach to human weakness must be different to one who has looked at sin from Gethsemani.

ONLY by entering into the sufferings of Christ, then, do we enter into the sufferings of man. This is compassion in its fullest sense, in its twofold direction. There can be surely no higher title given to Mary than that of Mother of Compassion. Since in the calendar of the Church we have reached the month of Mary we can examine for a moment the co-suffering of our Lady, relating our conclusions to the attitude of the priest towards his flock. En' trusted with the care of mankind, Mary became mother of the whole man—man weakened by original sin, tempted to actual sin, broken by the suffering of having sinned. More closely identified with her Divine Son than any other, Mary came closer than any other to the sinless, accepted, understanding and loving 'guilt' of Christ in the Garden. If the relationship between any mother and any son is intuitive, the relationship between this Mother and this Son leaves no possible room for misunderstanding or non-co-operation. Consequently if Christ enters into the wayward heart of man, Mary does the same. Mother of the Man Christ, she is mother of His mystical body, and the mystical body is still being tempted and tortured as the actual Body was tempted and tortured on Maundy Thursday. It is perhaps our tendency to imagine that the Immaculate Conception puts Mary so far outside the common weakness as to let her see sin only as it were academically: pitied, yes, but because never experienced not fully understood. Far from making her less understanding of sin, the Immaculate Conception makes her more so. Where in the rest of us sin blunts our sensibilities —causing us to condone, certainly, but not always to compassionate in its purest sense—in Mary the sensibilities are in any case all the sharper, and there has never been anything to blunt their edge. Her sympathy for the sinner is not less human than ours but more human; not theoretical or notional but actual and real.

APPLY all this now to the compassion which we, as priests, must show to those who come to us as penitents. It is not simply a matter of forgiving those who have sinned—most of us can manage that without great difficulty—but of 'presenting every man perfect in Christ Jesus.' For this we *have* to possess sympathy, for this we *have* to exercise endless patience, confidence, tact. With Christ we have to enter into the minds of men and share their difficulties. The allowances which we shall be called upon to make will seem out of all proportion to human reason, to worldly convention, to common prudence. People will bore us, misquote us, let us down, show us a hideous ingratitude and quite fail to benefit by the advice which we give them, but we must nevertheless go on trying to do Christ's and Mary's work in them. So long as there are people who need to lean, we must be there to be leaned on.

FOR us priests the principle of dealing with souls is unqualified: we interest ourselves, as Christ did, in all who stray into our lives; we devote to them as much of ourselves and of our time as they may need so that they may in turn devote themselves to Christ. It is a selfless and often a thankless purpose, but then God has called us to a vocation which is meant to be selfless and—though not entirely even in this life—thankless. Men whose work is with material things may expect material results: we whose work is to guide the minds and wills of men must expect to operate largely in the dark, must expect to feel the sense of insufficiency and crushing failure. Men are free to follow or reject what we tell them, so of course we miss the assurance that our work for their souls is successful. We should always be reminding ourselves that those to whom we are useless are precisely those for whom Christ must feel a special responsibility. Provided we have nothing with which to reproach ourselves, He can be relied upon to work direct. 'Think what an office is that of priests,' says St. Vincent de Paul, 'who are bound to guide souls of which God alone knows the movements. *Ars artium, regimen animarum.* This was the employment of the Son of God when He was on earth. To show us that for the work of helping souls we have more than our own practical judgment to rely upon, St. Vincent goes on to ask: 'What means are to be employed in order to carry out this office of opposing the torrent of vices and inspiring a people with a love for Christian virtue? Surely there is nothing human in such an undertaking; it is the work of God . . . it is to continue the work begun by Jesus Christ, and, furthermore, human industry can here do nothing but spoil it all if God be not a sharer in the work. Neither philo'sophy, nor theology, nor sermons operate on souls: Jesus Christ must work with us or we with Him. Let us work with Him and let Him work in us. Let us speak as He spoke and in His spirit.'[1]

On the eve of Solomon's consecration as King, the Lord invited His servant to make any request he wished. I will grant you whatever you want, said the Lord, be it peace or wealth or triumph in battle . . . all you have to do is to choose. But Solomon asked for none of these things: 'Give

[1] *Saint Vincent de Paul* by Father Leonard, p. 29.

unto me an understanding heart' was his prayer, 'with which to judge Your people.' We priests might do well, every day of our lives in the Mass, to ask for the same favour. Whether many or few of God's people come to us for judgment we shall need the gift of understanding. Is it said of us, 'I could never go to confession to him; he wouldn't understand'? Why, even the pagans know the beauty of compassion: 'having tasted sorrow'—so Dido to Æneas—'I have learned to compassionate the sorrowing.'

6

THE SACRIFICING PRIESTHOOD

IL n'y a rien de plus grand dans l'univers que Jésus Christ, says Bossuet, *il n'y a rien de plus grand dans Jésus Christ que son sacrifice.* If every-thing in our Lord's life led up to Calvary, every-thing in the priest's life leads up to the Mass. The trouble is for most of us that we get the balance wrong: the Mass takes half an hour, and the other claims upon us go on for the rest of the day. But to have the Mass rightly placed in our lives is to have the effects of the Mass going on all day and the claims upon us coming under cover of its grace. Such is the ideal, such is the theory. In order to reach up to the ideal, the priest must make very sure of the practical. The morning Mass must *be* the most important act of the day: must be pre-pared for, performed with the strictest care, allowed a reasonable thanksgiving. St. John Chrysostom says in his pleasantly explosive man-ner that God 'prefers the barking of dogs to the praises of man that are uttered in an unbecoming manner.' If we had only a lively enough sense of the Mass's apostolic force—let alone of its impact upon our own souls—there would be no question of our saying it in an unbecoming manner. St. Vincent de Paul tells how on one occasion when he was at St. Germain-en-Laye he saw seven or eight priests all saying Mass differently. 'It was enough to make a person weep. But now, God be praised, the Divine Goodness has remedied the disorder.' Not, alas, altogether; persons might still weep at the way in which some of us say Mass.

For a layman the outward sameness of the daily Mass might reasonably be an excuse for a certain boredom in its attendance. But for the priest, who not only attends but actively participates in the sacrifice of Christ, there should not be this diffi-culty. The power of the Church's liturgy as it varies from day to day should be strong enough— even if the theological aspect of it has grown so familiar to the mind of the celebrant as to make no immediate appeal—to carry the soul along in its tremendous movement. The priest is liturgically

D

undernourished if it does not. Even apart from the words of the Missal which must remind him in every paragraph of the significance and implication of the sacrifice, there are the ceremonies and the actual forms used in its celebration which bring the added weight of an unmistakable but almost in-exhaustible symbolism into play. Whatever it is for the layman (and happily the idea of the faith-ful actively co-operating with Christ, Priest and Victim, in the Mass is more and more taking hold) the Mass invites of the priest a total offering of himself with the elements to be consecrated, a real and positive reproduction of Christ's dis-positions both at the Last Supper and on Calvary.

SINCE in our series of considerations on the priest-hood we have reached the season of Corpus Christi, a few notes on the incidental symbolism contained in the Mass might not be out of place. The more fundamental symbols are familiar to us —how the corporate character of eucharistic wor-ship is shown in the *oblata* of bread and wine (each being the product of separate entities: in the one case the ears of wheat together making up the single host, in the other the grapes losing their separate existence in the wine offered from the chalice)—but even in the apparently accidental details are to be found suggestions of the same truths. The candles on the altar, for example, deriving their material from the collected result of countless individual efforts . . . and giving their light, moreover, by the act of sacrificing them-selves. The altar-stone, again, consecrated by means of oil (a corporate product once more) and sealed with the relics of separate, yet now com-bined, martyrdoms. If it be a High Mass there is the incense to point the same moral—namely that though we may be hard and angular by nature, we mingle with other hard and angular entities in giving common worship to God. In the thurible the bitter is made sweet. In the thurible, as in the case of the candle on the altar and the salt in the gospel, the incense loses its life—its own private life—so that it may give what is required of it to the element which it is designed to serve. Sacrifice, always sacrifice. The seed dying that it may live. The soul losing itself in one life and finding itself —its real and finished self—in another. If a priest does not come away from the altar more ready

each morning to live his day as if on the paten it
is not the Mass's fault.

'BUT no sooner do I get back to the sacristy,' the
pastor of souls will object, 'than I am expected to
answer questions, and the daily blinding sandstorm
of petty little importances begins.' With all respect
and humility it is here suggested that, excepting
only such manifestly spiritual duties as taking Holy
Communion to the sick, no outward affairs whatever should be allowed to interfere with the quar-
ter of an hour after Mass. At *least* this amount of
time is needed if the soul is to breathe properly :
without it the lungs of the spirit will remain
cramped all day. Just as architectural masterpieces
do not normally rise sheer from the sidewalk and
are not wedged in between a whole lot of other
houses, so neither should the Mass be exposed
immediately to the street nor sandwiched between
lesser occupations. In England our cathedrals are
fronted and flanked by lawns of cut grass which
are called a 'close.' The town is kept at bay; there
is no traffic across the close. The priest must con-
trive to lay down a 'close' round his Mass: no

traffic, no business; before and after Mass—silence. The alternative is spiritual suffocation. With the eucharistic part of his day safeguarded and allowed to give impetus to his charity, the priest will be able to meet the demands made upon him by his parish, by his studies, by his correspondence. Steeped in the spirit of his Mass he will be able to take the Mass with him into his work. Otherwise he will be a priest only when he wears his vestments. To be a priest throughout the day is difficult enough in any case, but it is doubly so if he starts off as a quick-change artist.

'BUT I do all that you recommend,' may be the objection, 'and still I find that from breakfast till going to bed the claims of outward duty so assert themselves as to leave the spiritual duties to be fitted in at odd moments.' Temporal cares are always cited against spiritual obligations, and nearly always the spiritual is seen to give way to the temporal. But after all it is we who make our duties temporal. If we thought less of duties and more of the way they might be done, we would not be bothered by the label 'temporal.' We are surrounded by the spiritual from morning to night if we only take the trouble to look.

'YES, but you don't have to do accounts, coach teams, produce light musicals, run a school. . . .' Try the symbolism of the Mass on all these things and see what happens. Look upon them as so many particles scooped onto the paten and dropped into the chalice. Say to our Lord both during Mass and during the day, 'These crumbs are Yours, they are part of Your Body. . . . I put them back where they belong.' As for fitting in the Divine Office, the time of mental prayer, the rosary and the visit to the Blessed Sacrament, here again we get our cue from the action of the Holy Sacrifice. Does not the celebrant at High Mass have to fit in the Epistle and Gospel while something else is being done in the sanctuary? At the spaces of the *Memento* which interrupt the otherwise unbroken sequence of the Mass, does he not redirect, as he redirects during those tip-and-run prayers which break into the sequence of his day, the arrow of his intention? Souls of the living and the dead referred to God at Mass: work for the Church referred to God at intervals during the day. The principle is much the same.

As we stand at the altar, then, so shall we stand for the rest of the day. We are facing the sacred species; everything else—relatively important but not as infinitely vital as what is going on in front of us—is being taken care of *in plano* behind us.

7

THE MILITANT PRIESTHOOD

IN the foregoing essay we saw that the source of the priest's active ministry lay in the Mass. The Mass is his first consideration as an apostle—let alone as a man of prayer. 'The primary function of the priesthood has for its object the *corpus Christi verum*,' says St. Thomas, 'the secondary the *corpus Christi mysticum;* the second depends upon the first.' Having dealt with the sacrificial side of the priest's life we turn naturally to examine the apostolic. But always it must be remembered that the two go together: there is no conflict: the altar-priest and the pulpit-priest are one. You do not have to serve two masters; you serve one Master in two ways. If upon you lies the responsibility of bringing others to perfection, of 'presenting every man perfect in Christ Jesus,' you may not satisfy your obligation merely from the predella. 'Souls come to us priests,' says Père

Ginhac, 'in order to find Jesus. Give them Jesus, and in their turn they will give Him to their child- ren, to their parish, to all with whom they come in contact.' Not only must we have Him; we must be prepared to share Him, show Him, open men's eyes to what He is really like. Diocesan clergy, then, and those religious who belong to active orders, have the vocation and duty to leave the precincts of the temple and mingle with the tribes. They even have the call, not the whole time but some of the time, to do battle in defence of the Faith. A percentage of them, the best, have the call to martyrdom. Priests belong, if any do, to the Church Militant. Not to a Church quiescent, still less to a Church dormant. It is the gift of the Holy Spirit, coming upon our first fathers at Pentecost, that provides priests with their vocational resilience.

IF, as St. Bernardine of Siena says, 'the power of the priesthood is as the power of the Divine Per- sons,' then by the sacrament of Holy Orders a more abundant, or at all events a more potentially effective, grace of Indwelling is conveyed. 'You

are fulfilling the office of the Holy Spirit,' writes
St. Vincent to a fellow priest, 'to whom alone it is
given to enlighten men's minds and inflame their
hearts. Or rather it is the Holy sanctifying Spirit
Himself who does so through you.' Now the doctrine of Divine Indwelling means surely this,
that not only is Christ's spirit so within the soul
as increasingly to draw the human thoughts,
desires, affections and intentions into conformity
with His own mind, but that the soul, living in and
for God, is able to transmit to others without loss
to its inward union the graces of which it is now
the human channel. God could have chosen to
work directly upon souls, but normally He chooses
to make use of human agents. The reason why no
loss is sustained, but on the contrary amassed, by
the human agent, operating as it were away from
his base and among the distractions of the active
life, is that he is re-enacting the ministry of Christ.
Christ lost nothing in leaving His Father's will at
Nazareth in order to do His Father's will on the
roads and in the cities. For us the tendency is to
make for the roads and cities before the Divine Indwelling has declared the time ripe for outward
action.

It is here that obedience comes to the rescue. So long as the priest does not press for new assignments, or in any way manœuvre towards them, but waits for the word from authority he need not have the least worry. His business is to attend to the Divine Indwelling; the Divine Mission can be taken up when it comes along. It is for the secular priest, no less than for the religious, to follow the will of his superior and not to get in front and pull.

Given, then, the mandate to go into the world and preach the Gospel to every creature, the priest must be particularly careful about two things: success and failure. (He must be careful about a number of other things as well—some of which will be indicated as this series develops.) He must realize, with the Apostles after Pentecost, that the response he meets with is the response of the soul to Christ. Detachment from the purely personal element in his work is an absolute necessity to the resulting good. All the time he is meant to be perfecting souls in Christ, forming Christ in men's souls, labouring for the Word and not for the applause which greets the Word. There is nothing that stifles the spirit of Pentecost so surely as a courted popularity. The success that is not founded on indifference to success is an ephemeral affair; the priest who shines by the light of his natural gift, and not by reason of the supernatural life he is trying to lead, is a cardboard star. 'Woe to them,' says St. Bernard, 'who merely shine.' Failure, in the same way, is to be taken in the priest's stride. The Godward direction of the work, the spiritual motive and effort, the accompanying mortification (or charity or patience or trust or any other virtue which has been brought into play) . . . all these things are not wasted merely because the final result has been a disappointment instead of a triumph. The house that burns down on the day of its completion does not nullify, or even waste, the labour that went into building it. Outward failure resulting from long and conscientious effort denotes no more than that God has seen fit to dis´ pense with the part of the work which, to Him apparently, matters least. The material of the sac´ rifice is consumed; it is the fact of the holocaust that matters. Seen against the Passion of Christ, no failure should have power to discourage. Failure, like the Cross itself, is not a punishment but a privilege.

THUS the work of the priest (whether in the pulpit, in the confessional, in his correspondence or in his instruction of converts and children) is to light up the paths that lead to God—while himself remaining suspicious of publicity, unafraid of frustration. 'It is a greater thing to give light,' says St. Thomas in a famous passage, 'than merely to see light oneself.' But he goes on at once to say that 'it is a greater thing to contemplate in order to hand on the fruits of one's contemplation to others than to contemplate alone.'[1] Back again always at the balance between the inward and the outward charity; back again always at moving the fingers of Martha with the mind of Mary.

AT this point we leave the ordinary run of pastoral life for a consideration of the specifically militant. It is not enough, accordingly, to confine our duty to a holding operation; we have more to do than

[1] *Sum. Theol.*, II-II, Q. clxxxii, art. i.

prevent our flocks diminishing. We must know how, when, and what to attack. The moment we lose our zest for evangelization, we find ourselves falling back upon prepared positions. If our Lord pointed to the highways and byways, if He spoke of fields white for harvest, if He wanted His disciples to be fishers of men and shepherds of sheep that have gone astray, it is a sad unconcern that keeps priests tethered to their desks, their armchairs, and their television. The opportunity for pressing the Catholic claim is as varied now as it has ever been. If the Apostles went out from the cenacle at Pentecost to the market-place, the courthouse, and to death, we of this generation should not be slow, given the dispositions outlined above, to mount the platform, to importune the editorial office, to bring what influence we can to bear upon the radio and screen. The Holy Spirit must grieve to hear the formula 'it is none of my business.' Is it none of my business that error goes uncorrected, that the Word is drowned, that corrupting literature is accessible to the young? 'It's for the hierarchy, not for me, to move . . . am I my brother's keeper? . . . I don't hold with this priest-worker movement . . . we've managed well enough up till now.' These are evasions, escapes, admissions of defeat. Leave your defence' mechanisms for a moment and read what our Lord said when He sent out the twelve and the seventy' two; read the Acts and see how St. Paul went about his job; read any period of Church history. The Christian tradition is a combative tradition. The Church does not have to apologize for its existence. If history, from St. Augustine's day to this, proves anything about Christianity it proves these two things: first, that where religion is preached without the backing of the Cross you get heresy; second, that where power is given more attention than prayer you get apathy. We should, during this time of Pentecost especially, invoke the Holy Spirit *qui docet manus meas ad proelium*. In His Spirit we shall preach Christ crucified by living Christ crucified; and in carrying the truth to a bewildered and materialistic world we shall be able to risk ridicule, jealousy, misrepresentation, and—if we are among the favoured—persecution and death.

8

THE PREACHING PRIESTHOOD

STILL under cover of the Pentecostal season we come to the question of our responsibility as 'voices of the Word.' If the first Whitsunday sent out the Apostles to preach and teach—as well as to offer sacrifice and baptize—the day of our ordination launches us on identically the same mission. As subdeacons and deacons we have received the book of the Gospels from the bishop; as priests we have received the commission to hand that book on to others and to explain it. 'Let your teaching be a spiritual remedy for God's people' are the words addressed to the ordinand, 'that both by preaching and example you may build up the household of God.' A fisherman one day, a preacher the next: yesterday a clerical student, today an exponent of the word of God. And if the word of God it not to return to God void, the preacher of the word must put into its exposition all that God has given to him in the way of nature and grace.

'It is the duty of a pastor,' says St. Gregory in one of his letters,[1] 'to have in his thoughts constantly the ministry of preaching, pondering with the most earnest fear those words of our Lord: Trade till I come.' St. Gregory, it might here be noted, rarely uses the word *praedicare;* nearly always his word is *docere.* This is significant, because though the whole purpose of his *Regula Pastoralis* is to make pastors speak effectively to their flocks, his empha- sis is on the moral aspect of the duty rather than on the method to be employed. Indeed he is not interested in questions of rhetoric or any of the tricks of production. St. Gregory's preoccupation throughout the *Regula Pastoralis* (which will be taken as our principal authority for this section of the work in hand) is one of disposition: first how to get the disposition of the pastor right, second how to dispose the flock to listen. For St. Gregory the problem is simply this: who can expect to spread the Gospel whose private life is not in keep- ing with his spoken utterance or who does not

[1] Lib. 11, Ep. 39, ad Dominicum Episcopum.

E

study and try to understand the human beings with whom he has to deal? The pastor's office is there-fore not only *summa dicere*—to speak things of supreme moment—but *summa monstrare*—to show by his conduct that they are supremely momen-tous to him. This is only another way of saying what we find in the opening prayer of the ordina-tion ceremony: *imitare quod tractas*. All so many reminders—as if we needed reminding—of the priest's daily summons to be one with his proto-type in the Mass: *hostiam puram, hostiam sanc-tam, hostiam immaculatam*.

When we have read up what the spiritual writers, psychologists, orators, and instructors in elocution have to say about it, we realize with a certain relief that the work of carrying conviction by means of the publicly spoken word is conditioned by the simple quality of truth. If the matter is true and if the man propounding it is true—that is to say if he is sincerely following what he conceives to be his nature and his vocation—there is every reason to believe that the hearers will benefit by what is said. Since for the moment it is not our

hearer's dispositions but our own that we are considering, and since our present purpose is a more
practical one than St. Gregory's in the *Regula
Pastoralis,* we may treat the priest's work of
preaching under three heads: how he is to prepare
for it, what he is to say, and whether there is anything he may do towards cultivating a delivery.

The priest, not merely during his time of training
in the seminary but throughout his whole life, is
fitting himself both to penetrate deeper and deeper
into the fundamental counsels contained in the
mysteries of the Incarnation and Atonement, and
to distribute the fruits of his study and experience
to a more or less purblind world. The priest pre-
pares for his office of preaching, as he should prepare for every sermon that he preaches, by seeing
himself as no more than the messenger of God and
the ambassador of Christ. 'We speak as from
God,' says St. Paul to the Corinthians, and before
God.' The truths that the priest learns from the
Holy Spirit he imparts—just as Elias imparted
after he had learned on Horeb, and Moses
imparted after he had learned on Sinai—to the

multitudes in the plain. But all the time he is in
the sight of God and will have to render an account
of his imparting. He mounts the pulpit as a prophet
to teach, direct, admonish and exhort those souls
for whom Christ died. *Declaratio sermonum
tuorum illuminat et intellectum dat parvulis; os
meum aperui, et attraxi spiritum.* We recite these
verses from the breviary, but do we ever relate
their thought to the main work which we are
expected to do for souls? Do we face the fact
that the words of our sermons must be God's
words, that they are designed to give light
and understanding? What powers we have, we
priests! And also what responsibilities and temptations in our preaching. 'The ear that heard me
blessed me' says, surely in the person of every
priest, the holy man Job, 'and the eye that saw me
gave witness to me. Because I had delivered the
poor man that cried out. The blessing of him that
was ready to perish came upon me, and I com-
forted the heart of the widow. I was an eye to the
blind and a foot to the lame. They that heard me
waited for my sentence, and being attentive held
their peace at my counsel. To my words they durst
add nothing, and my speech dropped upon them.'

There are few things more humbling, and in some ways more frightening, than being listened to and believed. We priests must handle the word of God with fear.

It would seem, then, that the qualities to be looked for in the preacher are humility, sincerity, and the desire to bring souls straight to God. Next comes the question as to where to begin and what to say. Surely the first and last subject for the Christian priest to preach about is Christ. 'I preach Christ and Him crucified,' was St. Paul's proudest boast, and it should be ours as well. Nevertheless from the pulpits of Catholic churches one hears philosophy, culture, education, hygiene and heaven knows what else before one can catch an echo of the Gospel. Time and time again the moral and spiritual development of the faithful is sacrificed to their purely natural well-being. The social services can be preached from the platform; for heaven's sake leave the pulpit free for the Gospel. What if the time which it took our Lord to preach the Sermon on the Mount had been spent in asking for money, in explaining architect's plans, in giving statistics about conversions and school-attendance, in urging the Jews to sing up in their choir practice and advising them how to use their vote? And the Sermon on the Mount has never really come to an end: it can be continued by us every time we get up to speak in church. Not even by us but by Christ Himself, speaking through our lips.

LASTLY there is the question as to *how* we preach, the manner we employ. Provided we make sure of the matter and the motive, we need not be greatly exercised about the manner. Again it is a question of being genuinely oneself and not acting a part. To become a slave to a system is as bad for preaching as to become a slave to a sermon book or even to one's own notes. There are practical dangers to be avoided—such as mannerisms, witticisms, a too frequent use of quotation—but because a person's style is such a highly individual thing and must be evolved in the course of his experience, there are few, if any, positive rules which will be found helpful. The principle of sincerity will be further examined in the ensuing study, and if the conclusions arrived at in connection with the priest's work of spiritual direction are applied equally to his work of preaching—the preacher, after all, is the spiritual director of the many—then the mere matter of delivery, the mechanism of it, will be seen to pale into relative insignificance.

To conclude. The whole aim of the preaching apostle might be stated in a text from St. Augustine: *ut veritas pateat, veritas placeat, veritas moveat.*[1] (And of these the middle clause is nothing like as important as the other two.) If the truth, as handled by us, be either muddled or unmoving—if we have either wrapped it up too much with smart thinking or thrown it to our hearers without personal feeling—a terrible reproach will be ours. On the day of our ordination we heard these words: 'The Lord chose seventy-two and sent them forth to preach before Him, thus teaching by word and example that the ministers of His Church should be perfect in faith and action.' Of all our actions as ministers of God, the act of repeating His word comes nearest in importance to that of repeating His sacrifice and conferring His sacrament. *Imitare quod tractas*— this is the code of the priestly vocation.

[1] De Doct. Christiana I, 4.

9

THE DIRECTING PRIESTHOOD

IN some ways the duty of directing the faithful is a more difficult obligation for a priest to fulfil than that of preaching. For one thing he will find that a high percentage of his fellow priests will not admit its necessity. That he will have to preach is a horror which the student has faced since his first day in the seminary and before. That he will hear confessions is again part of the general under-taking. But that souls will come to him for guid-ance in prayer and the ways of the spirit is not always allowed for, not always prepared for, not always thought to be a good thing. Seen to be variously interpreted, the obligation is then brushed aside. Neglected obligations tend to con-form to a sequence: belittlement, denial, attack. If the paragraphs which follow are couched in strong terms it is because direction, both inside the confessional and out of it, is felt to be a respon-sibility which is laid upon every priest with the grace of ordination and one moreover which is in need of restoration. For a priest to say that he is no good at it and that he is unworthy to give it is one thing—though as we shall see a completely misconceived thing—but either to say that there is no occasion to provide spiritual direction or to attack the practice as a waste of time, as minister-ing to the vanity of old ladies, as creating an atmos-phere conducive to fase mysticism, is contrary to the mind of the Church and its traditional usage.

In his book *The Spiritual Director* Father Gabriel make the position perfectly clear. Quoting Pope Leo XIII who declared it to be a 'common law of Providence that souls should be led to the loftier spiritual heights through being helped by other men' Father Gabriel would claim that the question is not open to personal opinion at all. Souls are groping in the darkness; true spirituality is the only thing that will satisfy them; the need is not being adequately met. Whose fault is that? Priests are all too ready to imagine that if they have done their duty by dogmatic and moral theology they can leave ascetical and mystical theology to those who have a taste for these things and who can teach from their own experience. To argue thus

F

is not an act of humility but an act of evasion. Granted that a director is helpful to souls in the measure that he has himself been through the trials which are put to him, it is at least a preparation towards being helpful that he should read up the subject and get himself acquainted with the ex' perience of the saints. From having studied the authorities it will be not such a long step towards walking in their footsteps. Cultivating a taste for spiritual literature is like cultivating a taste for any other kind of literature: you have to read it. St. Teresa, St. John of the Cross, the author of *The Cloud,* Walter Hilton, de Caussade . . . these are the theologians whom an increasing number of penitents are hungering to know. How can the be' wildered flock find an entry to such pastures if the shepherds are constantly shrugging their shoulders and saying that the hills are out of reach?

THE priest does not exist solely to keep his peni' tents out of mortal sin and to help them up again when they have fallen into it. He exists in order to sanctify them . . . and in doing so to sanctify himself and give a particular kind of glory to God.

If God is glorified by the sacrifice offered by His priests, He is glorified also by the special sort of assistance which it is in the power of priests to give. The layman is the amateur, the priest is the expert. 'Expert?' you say in horrified humility, 'but some of the laymen who come to me are far more experienced in the life of prayer than I am . . . it is I who am the amateur.' Quite so, but why? Is it not because the layman has made more of his lay graces than you of your priestly ones? The layman may well be advancing more rapidly in the way of perfection than you are, but this— except in so far as it should act as an additional spur to your endeavour—is not the point. The point is that the priest is the professional, the leader, the director, and however insufficient he may feel himself to be by reason of quite obvious shortcomings, he is, by reason of his state, qualified to direct. If he is not qualified, if he is genuinely unequal to the task, there is something gravely wrong which needs attending to.

Suppose a penitent in the confessional finds great difficulty in producing matter for absolution and at the same time begs to be brought nearer to God;

suppose someone who has been recently married is eager to hear more about the counsels of perfec-tion with regard to the Sacrament of Matrimony and less about the evils which threaten it; suppose a man or woman in business is troubled at not be-ing able to maintain the practice of the presence of God during office hours and wants know why meditation books do not help. Does the confessor have to admit that he is familiar enough with the problems of drunkards and adulterers but that this sort of thing is beyond him? Is he content to fall back on the formula, that last plank of the con-fessional box, along which so many puzzled and well-intentioned souls are ushered back into the aisle: 'You just have to try your best, that's all, and leave the result in God's hands'?

As we saw in the question of preaching, so we see now in the question of giving advice in the con-fessional or by correspondence: a man has to be himself, but the self must be responsive to the lightest touch of grace. It is personal holiness, more than learning or a ready flow of words, that is going to tell in the end. Whether in the pulpit or in private conversation, the one thing fatal to the work of direction is an assumed sanctity. For one thing it is as easily detected and exposed as an assumed learning or an assumed wit. But the idiom of the saints does not have to be learned; it is the quality of sanctity that has to be reproduced. And it is this, in the last analysis, which deters the majority of priests from the apostolate of direction : they know that the souls who come to them for help are a challenge. Let them be a challenge, let their very need call our bluff, let us come away ashamed both of our ignorance regarding the subjects raised and of our lack of personal experience.

To conclude. Our words of advice are not expected to be infallible pronouncements—it would be very bad for us if they were—but they are expected to be forthcoming when required. In the *Regula Pastoralis* St. Gregory says that just as those whose function it was in the Old Law (Exodus 25) to be ready for the carrying of the Ark of the Covenant from one place to another— which they did by means of rods inserted into rings which stood out from the sides of the Ark—so the

Church's pastors, constant in their study of Scripture and holy reading, must always be ready to do their share of lifting. The sacred burden of teaching, whether of dogma or morals or pure spirituality, is overlaid with the gold of perfect practice. St. Gregory goes on to note that the rods which have been passed through the rings may never be withdrawn: there is to be no dilettante eclecticism in our application to supernatural things.

'THE divine word is a sacrament in which the priest has a more personal efficacy than anyone else,' says St. Peter Fourier, 'and one which demands on his part a great labour and a great respect.' So it looks as if there is no escape: labour, personal holiness, identification with Christ whose words flow through us. 'With thee is the fountain of life,' we say with the Psalmist, 'and in thy light we shall see light.' It ought not to be difficult for the priest, drawing from the inexhaustible sources at his disposal, to find the right course to suggest. At least he can recommend the right authorities to be studied. If his own principal authority is Christ, and if he makes it his primary object to draw souls to Christ, he has little to fear. 'This is eternal life, that they may know Thee, the only true God': this is the knowledge which we are called out of the unbelieving world to teach. Our own minds nourished by the Gospels, the Fathers, the traditional spiritual literature of the Church, we who are called *pastores* will be able to live up to our name by feeding the flocks of Christ. 'There is a wisdom which comes from above,' says St. Thomas,[1] 'which judges divine things in virtue of a certain affinity with them. This wisdom is a gift of the Holy Ghost . . . through it a man becomes perfect in divine things, not only by learn-ing about them but also by experiencing them.' Of all gifts granted to priests, this is possibly the most neglected. It should not be only the canonized saints who can say with St. Hilary: 'I acknow-ledge that I owe my life's occupation to God, so that every word and thought of mine may speak of Him.'

[1]*Sum. Theol.*, II-II, Q. xlv,

10

THE ACCESSIBLE PRIESTHOOD

THERE are some truths, some ways of acting, some attitudes of mind which are hardly worth writing about. Experience—particularly the experience of having made mistakes—reveals far more to the soul than the mere reading of articles. What follows, therefore, will be found virtually useless—except insofar as it warns the soul where to look for its pitfalls.

The question under review is the tight-rope one of walking between an excess of concern for souls on the one hand and an excess of indifference towards souls on the other. St. Macarius tells us that the pastor must 'sit as in the theatre and see what goes on upon the stage . . . while interiorly conversing with God.' He must cultivate such spiritual detachment that his approach to souls is impersonal : he sees them from the auditorium. He prays for the players, but avoids getting entangled in the plot. Clearly St. Macarius is steering for safety. Most priests with the care of souls would today feel that St. Macarius was wrong, and that the course to follow would be to get onto the stage as soon as possible after ordination and mix with the performers . . . or at least to hang about in the wings and to catch them for a talk about their religious duties as they come behind the scenes.

In our doubt about the wisdom of St. Macarius we turn to our authority St. Gregory. In the fifth and sixth chapters of his *Regula Pastoralis* St. Gregory lays down his doctrine of accessibility. *Singulis compassione proximus* is to be the extent of the priest's human sympathy. The interest which he is to take in the lives of those entrusted to him is no academic thing: he is to feel sympathy —not merely feign it and show pity—for his fellow men. The flock must be made to know that here is a father who is acutely sensitive to the sufferings, temptations, weaknesses, follies of his children. Nothing distant and doctrinaire about this. St. Gregory, in his development of the idea, reminds the shepherd about the equal rights enjoyed by his sheep. Here surely, in this second part of the thesis, we see the corrective for which the followers of St. Macarius have doubtless been looking. Since it is only sin that has caused some men to be placed under others (runs St. Gregory's argument) so it must be Christian charity that causes all men to take their equal place before God and one another. *Now* the priest can sit in his stall and view the players on the stage. All are in the chorus . . . all are stars. The individual is of infinite worth; the whole company is made up of likenesses to Christ. All are playing the one part, Christ's. In applauding and loving those who play it well, as in excusing those who play it ill, the priest may never forget that it is primarily Christ's act. Christ's play, Christ's function—as Producer —to allot the praise and blame.

THE priest, then, has to remember two things: first, that it is no use getting so excited about the souls of his parish that he comes to look upon them as belonging more to him than to God; second, that because all souls are alike valuable to God it is not his own superior excellence that has placed him in his position of responsibility over others.

Cuncti qui praesunt, non in se potestatem debent ordinis sed aequalitatem pensare conditionis. They should think less of their status as priests and more of their state as souls: less of their dignity and more of their dependence: less of the authority which they possess and more of the Authority whence it derives. Unless the priest is class-oblivious in his service of others he inevitably judges them as social and not as spiritual beings. The soul is hidden in the class. In every civilization, however socialist, men fall readily into classes. Where at one time the main distinction was clear—the distinction between freemen and slaves—the divisions which have come with progress are now less clear. But they exist nevertheless, and are very real. The idea of caste, whether the aristocracy be one of blood or of money or of power, can become so extreme as to deny the essential implication of the Incarnation. An error which gives supernatural dignity to rulers is not likely to give even natural dignity to the ruled. Exaggeration in the rights enjoyed by one section of the community inevitably leads to a corresponding exaggeration in the wrongs endured by another. Though there can never be a classless

society, there can be a just order in the classes
which make up the society. If there cannot be
equality, there can at least be equity. And this
is where the Christian, all the more the priest,
comes in.

We preach the dignity of the ordinary individual.
However ordinary, he *is* individual. Every man's
soul has its own supernatural purpose—which is
every bit as important as the next man's. All are
heirs to eternal happiness, all are redeemed by the
blood of Christ. No human being comes into the
world for the convenience of another; each one
comes that he may belong to God from whom he
has his being. Thus if an obstacle—namely sin or
error, or a set of circumstances which disposes
towards sin or error—gets in the way of this supernatural purpose, it is the work of those responsible
for men's direction to go to all lengths in combat-
ing the evil. If the shepherd is to look after his
flock he must see the members of it not as flesh and
blood but as what they are in the sight of God.
He must work for them in the same way that he
prays for them: seeing them as classless, weak,

impulsive, at the apparent mercy of fashion and propaganda, sometimes painfully ungrateful, always a little uncompromising . . . *but infinitely worth while.*

ONE of the notes of twentieth-century Catholicism is the stress which is laid upon the sanctification of the commonplace. We have St. Teresa of Lisieux to thank for this. Not only the common-*place* but the common *person.* Again St. Teresa bears witness to the sacredness of what is not imme-diately seen. If the feast of a saint can give its character to a season, then we have come to a time in the liturgical year when the doctrines of St. Teresa deserve examination. In the light, then, of what is generally know as The Little Way, we can consider some of the consequences of the fore-going paragraphs as relating more directly to the ministry.

IN the first place a priest is not priestly on special occasions—any more than a saint is saintly on special occasions—but is priestly all the time. It is, indeed, the unspecial occasions that are the test.

If he is unpriestly when he is off duty, there is reason to suspect the sincerity of his priestliness when he is on duty. And when is a priest *not* on duty? The quality of his service is not in the heroic moments but in the unheroic months—even years. The mountains may represent the triumphs, but it is the molehills which give us the practice. Mountains may be more challenging, but they are also more exhilarating. Nor do we stub our toes against mountains. Molehills are more our measure. This is not only St. Teresa's doctrine. The whole New Testament seems to teach, beginning with the example of Christ and Mary, that we do not mount to conquer but rather stoop to conquer. From the *Magnificat* to the *Consummatum est* the Gospel is the good news of the humble, the every-day. The Christian priest does not rescue the drowning by leaning over a deck-rail and throwing down a life-belt: he dives under their struggling bodies and carries them on his shoulders.

To conclude. The priest must find a just balance between the personal and the impersonal. He must know that when a man is fighting for life in the water it is not his home address that matters but his soul. In the waters of this world all are fighting for life, and we priests have taken an elaborate course in life-saving. The priest must be at everybody's call every day and every night. Accessibility, willingness to be used, readiness to risk misunderstanding, ingratitude, neglect, and the drawing of the completest blank among those whom one chiefly wished to impress and attract . . . these things are of the marrow of our vocation. Personal love for every soul: impersonal detachment from the response with which that love is met.

11

THE PRAYING PRIESTHOOD

A CERTAIN lecturer in dogmatic theology was both so swift and so uncertain in his delivery that the students who sat under him found the greatest difficulty in taking notes, or indeed in following the drift, of what he said. On a particu- larly bad morning—cries of 'Slower,' 'Louder,' 'Clearer' proving of no avail—a voice brought the course of this particular professor's lectures to an end by shouting 'You're not saying Mass now, Father.'

THERE are few surer rules in the spiritual life than that we are before men what we are towards God. If we pray as we are meant to be praying, we inevitably serve God's creatures as they are meant to be served. This is not to press the above story too far, and to claim that the priest who races and mumbles his Mass will come to speak inaudibly, but it does mean that if a man is at home in his Father's house he is safely at home in other people's. It means that the priest who begins to neglect the direct, and interior, worship of God will give himself away in his work for souls. The words 'direct and interior' are here deliberately chosen. Indirect and exterior expressions of worship—such as pilgrimages, ceremonial occasions, and so on—are not enough. The priest must work his way further into the Mass than the rubrics can take him, must read between the lines of the spiritual reading book until he comes to know the feel of God's will, must see in the psalms and lessons of the breviary a personal and secret appeal to his own soul. Not until he can look the challenge of the interior life in the face is he fit to embark upon the exterior. Not until his work for souls is informed by the work which is going on in his own soul can the ministry be either truly fruitful to the faithful or further productive of good in himself. 'To those who love God, all things work together for good.' Can we be said to love God—we priests anyway—if we do not seriously attempt to unite ourselves with Him in prayer?

G

And if we fail to do this, can the good works that we do be seriously accounted to us for good?

It is only the man of supernatural faith, which is tantamount to saying that it is only the man of prayer, who can see God's creation in anything like its true shape. Without prayer, without the focus of vision which gradually comes to one who is habitually trying to adapt his mind to the mind of the Prime Mover, creatures are seen simply as things moved—as pieces on the board. To the man who lives by faith—particularly of course to the saint, whose prayer takes him to the perfection of faith—created things are part of a pattern as existing in the mind of the Creator. Nothing hap'hazard here; no question of the unaccountable and the irresponsible. Where the materialist may feel free to arrange the given symbols on the squares to suit his pleasure or his policy, the man of prayer knows with the wisdom which his increasing faith is unfolding to him that all these contingencies are in fact dependent upon God, and that therefore he must learn from God, in prayer, how to handle them. The materialist philosophies are not so far removed from us: there is always the danger that we view the universe only from the outside. Starved of prayer we see plenty of secondary causes and a whole world of contingent effects; but what we need, if these outward circumstances are to have a meaning and to be fitted into a plan, is to see more of the working of the First Cause, God. A parish would have much to fear from the leadership of a priest who was scornful of the value of prayer.

APART altogether from the question of disedification—and sooner or later the faithful would come to know that their pastor never prayed except when it would be a mortal sin not to—there is, as we have suggested, this invisible and unconfessed materialism in the minds of those who should be revealing the will of God to souls who are looking for it. If practical common sense, experience, quickness of wit, useful connections, were all that were needed for the guidance of a congregation, why not set up an office and have done? Why have a confessional and a pulpit and a waiting room for private interviews? It is just because the

natural judgment of a politician or a youth leader
or a psychiatrist goes only a little way towards the
mind of God that the man of prayer, who is supposed to be going a much further way, has to be
called in. What an anomaly it is when the so-called
man of prayer is not a man of prayer at all, but a
man of works only. Without the light which comes
of prayer—and it is a light which the faithful are
entitled to see in their spiritual guides—layfolk up
and down the world are wastefully groping their
way in the darkness. In God's mercy the balance
is presumably somehow redressed: the flowing of
grace is not dependent upon this or that channel.
But this is not the point. The point is that we
priests are the appointed channels, and if we fail
in an essential—even though that failure is known
to God alone—our people fail in an essential. We
are all in it; we are part of the pattern; we are
moving beings owing existence and purpose to the
First Mover, God.

As in the earlier studies in this sequence we find
that it is once more a matter of relating the outward to the inward, the inward to the outward.

One of the encouraging features of contemporary spirituality is what might be called the return of the symbol. In the liturgy, in the study of psychology, in the application of Scripture, symbolism is at last coming into its own again. In the East, where the idea of contemplation has a stronger hold on men's minds, the created order has always taken second place: the inward has always seemed more important than the outward: Easterns have searched the outward for the inner meaning which must underlie the concrete appearance: hence the appreciation of symbolism. In the more hard-headed West, however, the concrete appearance of an entity is inclined to be identified in the mind with the entity itself—with its substance. With us the study of a thing tends to go no deeper than its surface . . . why bother to investigate further? This is death to symbolism. This is death to mysticism. This is death, ultimately, to faith and prayer and religion generally. Thus the revival of interest in the *meaning* of familiar forms is healthy: it is a return to a purer mentality. The child who asks why the grain of wheat looks so different from the field about to be harvested—and still more different from the loaf of bread he sees at breakfast or the Host he receives at Holy Communion—is nearer in his mental operation to the way in which God wants men to think than is either the scientist who can tell you the component parts of every different specimen in the corn category or the financier who can tell you how to make money out of it. So long as we want to know why life is what it is we are still open to the light: if we confine our examination to what matter consists of and how it can be turned to our advantage we may well miss the point of creation. It is when men miss the point of creation that they are in danger of destroying creation. Neither of these conditions would be possible if men prayed.

IF it is the function of the priest to draw men back to the truth from which they have strayed, the work will be done primarily by means of prayer. The prayer will communicate itself, multiply itself, give life. The life which prayer imparts is not merely a way of living: it is the Christ-life itself. Where the Greeks and Romans educated man so

that he was able to live in a certain way, Christianity educates a man so that he may think in a
certain way. We form in him the mind of Christ.
How can we even begin to do this unless we ourselves, the educators, have the mind of Christ? It
is not even enough to present the mind of Christ
—in the sense of exhibiting it and preaching about
it—when what the faithful are hungering for is the
sight of it in those who represent Him. Given
'other Christs' to work with and imitate, given
men among them who 'live now not they but
Christ liveth in them,' there is something for them
to strive after. Where men and women sense the
presence of prayer they head straight for it. Like
sanctity itself, of which it is both the preparation
and expression, prayer has a magnetic force beyond
all other forms of religion. The reason for this is
that in its exercise are contained the three theological virtues. And you can't ask much more of
any work than that it should combine at once faith,
hope, and charity.

12

THE VIGILANT PRIESTHOOD

THIS is a story which might be true but isn't,
and which might point a moral but doesn't.
There was once a parish priest who was so punc-
tual, and even so punctilious, about his duties that
members of the congregation, unaccustomed to
such regularity, would often ask him how he
managed it. 'We have never had Mass beginning
on time before,' they said . . . or 'Pastorals are
read on the right Sunday now' or 'Weddings and
funerals never seem to clash as they used to.'
Always the explanation was advanced: 'My assist-
ant takes care of it . . . my housekeeper has a
wonderful memory . . . my sacristan is a
treasure.' Then one day a very eloquent little man
came to the town, and Communism so swept the
parish that the people gave up coming to church.
All because neither the curate, nor the house

keeper, nor the sacristan had come across the Encyclicals.

PRIESTS who are content merely to mark time will find themselves doing it on a conveyor belt going backwards. There has to be an alertness about the priest's outlook which refuses to allow the enemies of Christianity, or even the competitors within the allegiance of Christianity, to hold the initiative. The priest's mind may not close on a certain date (say with the Vatican Council) and thereafter receive no further impression. His reading must keep pace, the subjects of his discussion must be open, his judgments must be *ad hoc* and not according to formula. Unless he is constantly on tiptoe to enlarge the stock of his ideas, he will never be wide enough awake to enlighten the minds of his parishioners.

Now if it is true that religion is meant to form moral human beings who will so live and die that they bring glory to God in both this world and the

next, then it must also be true that the official pro-
pagators must be habitually on the watch against
any new error—or old error under new impulse—
such as might threaten that moral and spiritual
purpose. This on the negative side. On the positive
side the apostles of truth must be equally ready to
pounce on the opportunities that are offered. 'You
mean I must preach sound doctrine,' says the priest
at this point, 'but, thanks, I do that already.' Certainly preach sound doctrine; but you must do
more in your preaching than reproduce in modern
language the sermons of St. Augustine, St. Bernard, Bossuet and Newman. You must present the
contemporary Church's answer to whatever the
contemporary challenge happens to be. The
Church is a living Church and you must live with
it. If you stopped growing when you left the seminary, you are now virtually a corpse. For example,
it is no good telling your people where the Arians
went wrong, when what they want to know is
where Leonard Feeney went wrong; it is no good
explaining the shades of difference between John
Wesley's approach and Savanarola's, when the
immediate difficulty is seeing any difference
between Mr. Graham's and Father Peyton's. Or

again, if Communism seeks to deprive the modern citizen of the highest object in the order of know-able being—namely God, the concept that explains the universe—then it is for you, as a spokesman for the cause of Christ, to establish that object in the minds and hearts of men in such a way that no attack will dislodge it. And you cannot do this without reading up the case.

Note that we have said 'in the minds and hearts of men.' The human intellect and the human will are alike moved by grace. But in either case the process is normally operated through the instru-mentality of other human intellects and other human wills. We priests, with our training and our prayer to help us, have the twofold duty of shep-herding human intellects toward the knowledge of truth, and of shepherding human wills toward the choosing of good. No wonder we are called shep-herds. Not enough to impart the knowledge by instruction: the will must be roused by exhorta-tion. Of the two, the second responsibility is more enduring than the first: the reason which sees a truth can be more or less depended upon to go on seeing it; the will which applies its knowledge must be kept at it till the choice of good becomes a habit and even second nature.

'I AM in labour,' says St. Paul to the Galatians, 'until I can see Christ's image formed in you.' It takes time. And the image is not of the dead Christ but the living Christ. The Christ who is today facing Communism, materialism, indifferentism, must today be formed in Christians. The faithful must come to think as Christ thinks: must have the mind of Christ on topics of the hour. How many people ask themselves what Christ thinks of television, atomic power, abstract art? Unless Christ's thought is reflected in our own, we are thinking to no purpose.

'Other foundation no man can lay but that which is laid,' St. Paul reminds the Corinthians, 'which is Christ Jesus.' The trouble about us priests is that we lay the foundation and then start building somewhere else. The faithful respond to the personal, the immediate; they get bored by the abstract, the remote. The ordinary Sunday - Mass - and-Holy-Communion Catholics are not vitally interested in wide concepts like 'the priesthood,' 'the religious life,' or even alas 'the Church.' What they are curious to know more about is this priest, this religious, this particular discipline or dispen- sation. It may show a faulty or frivolous attitude, but it is a very natural one. That is why it is easy to teach children about our Lord—He is a Person. That is why there is no difficulty about the Sermon on the Mount—Christ wants this and that done.

AND now to apply all this to shepherds, vigilance, and the priesthood. Priests are persons, and the faithful expect to see the person of the priest and the Person of Christ in some way identified. Not only have the faithful an instinctive ideal or pic- ture of Christ, but they have an instinctively idealized picture of the priest. It is not their fault, but his, if they measure the priest against Christ and see more difference than they bargained for. Sheep know the Good Shepherd and they know their own pastors. If they find their pastors un- concerned at the approach of wolves, if they come to feel that they and their fellow sheep are just so many units in the fold which can be fed from the pulpit on Sundays with any sort of hashed-up mess that can be collected at a moment's notice, if they have a shrewd suspicion that the study of their problems (which they themselves cannot resolve, and which they feel may admit of some spiritual solution) is of less importance to the shepherd of their souls than the returns which he has to make to the bishop (or than the sports news, or than the bridge dates, or than the new electric laundry in the presbytery) . . . and if, concluding that there is a discrepancy somewhere, they come to feel beyond a certain point of endurance the departure from the Gospel as they know it, they will cast about for other flocks and other shepherds.

In our liturgical cycle we have arrived at the season of Advent. Christmas should make us priests more conscious than ever of our office—with *pastor* meaning 'feeder' as well as 'shepherd.' It is as if Christmas were telling us to nourish, as well as guard, our flocks.

In the Nativity group there are oxen and asses but no wolves. Wolves, for this holy night, have either made a truce with man and cattle or else have been kept in the dark as to what is going on.

(There was peace, it may be remembered, throughout the Roman Empire at the time when Christ
was born.) But when the Christmas cave becomes
the ordinary stable again, we who have been wit-
nesses to the wonder of God's mercy return once
more to our state of alert. Christianity is from its
beginnings an underground movement: the state
of emergency, declared at the crisis of the Holy
Innocents and Herod's decree, has never been
lifted.

To conclude. Starting in the seminary where he
feels he is living in the cross between a barracks
and a kindergarten, the man who is called by God
to the ministry discovers that the actual thing is
like living in a combined watch-tower and clinic:
the priest is always either scanning the horizon or
offering his arm for a blood transfusion. The
danger is that he goes to sleep on the watch-tower
and lives on other people's blood in the clinic. To
correct these tendencies he must remember that the
wolves which prowl are live wolves and not dead
ones (duelling and slavery are wrong, but forget
about them—they are dead; and anyway they are

not as serious as their modern counterparts) . . .
and that the blood by which he lives, and which
he gives to others, is the blood of Christ. 'Christ is
our life,' says St. Paul in the person of every priest,
'that the life also of Jesus may be made manifest in
our mortal flesh.'